Simple and Speedy Microwave Cooking

C000040168

How many people make the most of their microwave? After the the appliance is all too often relegated to a minor role, used for softening butter, thawing frozen foods and baking potatoes, but little else. This book invites you to discover – or rediscover – the magic of the microwave. It concentrates on the foods the microwave likes best: vegetables cooked to perfection, their colours beautifully preserved; fish whose delicate flesh retains all the moisture and flavour nature intended; casseroles of tender meat cuts; superb steamed puddings and teabreads.

Microwave cookery, like stir frying, is so rapid that it demands a shift in thinking; preparation often takes more time than the actual cooking, so it is important to have all the ingredients to hand before you begin. For basic information – or a reminder of rules you may have forgotten – read the section on Microwave Know-how. Then choose a recipe, make any adjustments necessary for your own particular appliance and get switched on to microwave cookery. You've nothing to lose but time, effort and dirty saucepans!

NOTE The recipes in this book were tested in microwave ovens rated at 650-700 watts. Settings used are as follows: High (100 per cent); Medium High (70 per cent); Medium (50 per cent); Low (30 per cent) and Defrost (20 per cent). If your appliance is rated differently – or if the terms used differ from those on your microwave – consult your handbook for information on adjusting timings and settings. Timings given are for guidance only. It is not necessary to rotate dishes if your appliance is equipped with a turntable.

CONTENTS

MICROWAVE KNOW-HOW

Although the microwave has become almost as familiar as the frying pan, and prices have fallen steadily to make this an affordable – many would say essential – appliance in the well equipped kitchen, there are still many cooks who fail to make the most of their microwave. In the first flush of enthusiasm, many buyers have a 'microwave month', in which they try to cook everything the microwave way, only to discover that the appliance does not always meet their expectations. And there's the nub of the problem: there are culinary areas where the microwave excels and others where its particular method of cooking proves less successful. Value its advantages, accept its limitations, and the microwave will become an indispensable part of your kitchen.

How it works

Inside every microwave is a magnetron which converts electrical energy to high frequency microwaves. The microwaves cook, not by direct heat, but by causing the molecules in foods to vibrate so much that they literally rub up against each other; this causes friction which in turn produces intense heat. Rubbing the palms of your hands together vigorously produces a similar result (thankfully on a greatly reduced scale!).

Microwaves are attracted by the moisture, sugar or fat content of the food. They penetrate to a maximum depth of about 5 cm/2 inches; after that, the food is cooked by conducted heat, as in an ordinary oven.

Metal reflects microwaves, which has some advantages (the metal lining of the appliance, together with the metal screen in the glass door, reflects the microwaves back on to the food and at the same time prevents the microwaves from escaping) – and some drawbacks (with rare exceptions, you cannot cook in metal containers as the waves simply would not penetrate them).

What microwaves will penetrate, however, are glass, pottery, china, paper, wood and some plastics. The waves simply pass straight through these materials without heating them, which is why a bowl of food heated briefly in the microwave remains cool to the touch. Of course, the hot food will eventually heat the container, so you still need to take care when removing items from the microwave, especially if they have been microwaved for any length of time.

Because microwave cooking is a moist method, rather like steaming, items tend not to brown, nor will they become crisp. There are several ways around this, but it is something

to bear in mind if you want to avoid disappointment.

Plus points

Microwaves are economical; drawing about a quarter of the power required by one element in a conventional oven.

No preheating is required, saving time and energy.

A healthy diet is easier to achieve with the aid of a microwave. Many foods cook in their own juices, or with a small amount of water, so food retains its natural flavour and nutrients. It is not recommended that salt is added before cooking and you will find that improved flavour means that you need add less salt at table. Foods do not stick, so less fat is required.

Thawing is simplicity itself – a great asset when unexpected guests arrive or you have forgotten to shop.

Precooking is another advantage: start sausages and chicken drumsticks off in the microwave, then finish them on the barbecue, for a swift and safe summer meal.

The microwave saves washing up, as you can cook and serve in the same dish.

Food can be reheated in the microwave without loss of flavour or changes in texture.

The kitchen stays cool even when the temperature inside the oven is very high.

Finally, the appliance is itself easy to clean; wiping the inside of the cavity after every use only takes a moment and and stubborn spills will be easy to shift if a cup of water is boiled in the microwave for a few minutes.

Which microwave?

Microwaves range from small, simple appliances with two basic power settings, to sophisticated models with extra features, some of which automatically calculate the thawing or cooking time for certain foods or

Cook bacon on special microwave racks or place between sheets of paper towels to absorb fat and excess moisture while allowing steam to escape.

dishes. Power outputs vary; the recipes in this book are designed to be cooked in a conventional microwave (one which operates by microwave energy alone) with an output of 650-700 watts. Adjust timings if your microwave has a different rating, or if you are using a combination microwave. These appliances enable you to cook by microwave energy and conventional heat at the same time, thus neatly getting around the problem of browning and generally achieving excellent results.

Talk to other microwave users when deciding what to buy. Ask them which features they consider most valuable and use most often. You may well find that a middle-of-the-range microwave, with a simple range of settings (including a thawing facility) is all you need. It is useful to have a turntable as this promotes even cooking. Without it, you will need to remember to turn the food yourself from time to time. (Some manufacturers claim that the microwaves in their appliances are so efficiently distributed that a turntable is unnecessary.)

Read your handbook from cover to cover when you buy your appliance. If a cookbook is supplied, use it as a means of getting to know your particular microwave, and as a cross reference when cooking similar recipes from another book, such as this one. Because microwave cooking is so fast, small differences in timings can be quite significant. Check frequently: undercooking can easily be remedied; overcook something and it will be spoiled.

Equipment

It is not necessary to invest in a range of specific microwave cookware. Many of your everyday dishes will be perfectly suitable, including glass measuring jugs, ovenproof glass bowls, soufflé dishes and pie plates. Most pottery and china dishes and casseroles are also suitable.

Do not use metal containers, foil (except for shielding) or any items with metallic trim or metallic paint designs. Some microwaves allow a limited use of foil containers – check your handbook.

Paper can be used in various ways: as a lining or covering (greaseproof paper; paper towels; nonstick baking paper) or as a container for short-term cooking (paper cups; cupcake cups).

Roasting bags are very useful, especially for cooking vegetables. Remember to use rubber bands instead of metal ties, securing them loosely so that steam can escape. Microwave stretch wrap is ideal as a covering for bowls and dishes. Do not allow the wrap to touch the food and leave a gap or vent at the side for the steam. Alternatively, pierce the film in several places.

Boilable plastic bowls can be used for short term cooking, but may discolour if used for a highly coloured dish such as tomato sauce.

Wicker baskets can be used for very short periods, to reheat rolls, for instance.

In general, the microwave is not the best place for baking cakes, but some ring cakes and loaves work well. It is worth buying glass ring moulds and loaf dishes if you intend making a lot of cakes.

Browning dishes have a coating on the underside of the base to absorb microwave energy when preheated. The base becomes very hot and will brown and sear food. Alternatively, foods that require this treatment to seal in juices or improve appearance can be seared in a frying pan or finished off under the grill.

Special techniques

Arranging foods: Because microwaves penetrate the outer 5 cm/2 inches of food, items placed around the rim of a dish will be subjected to more energy than those in the centre. It is important to arrange foods so that the areas that will take longest to cook are placed near the outside of a dish, while tender areas are towards the centre. Broccoli spears for instance, should be placed in a circle with the heads pointing to the centre; chicken drumsticks should be arranged in a similar pattern, with the 'sticks' in the centre.

Piercing: Any food covered with a natural membrane or skin, such as jacket potatoes, must be pierced before microwaving. If this is not done, steam will build up and an explosion could occur. Never cook eggs in shells in a microwave except in a specially designed microwave egg boiler.

Stirring/Turning: Stirring is important to distribute the heat and ensure even cooking. Turning larger items, such as chicken breasts, is recommended for the same reason.

Rotating Dishes: If you do not have a turntable and the food you are cooking cannot be stirred or otherwise rearranged, give dishes a quarter or half-turn as and when recommended in individual recipes.

Shielding: This technique is sometimes used to protect parts of foods which are particularly thin and which might otherwise overcook, such as wing tips on poultry or the tail end of whole salmon. Check your handbook to ensure whether this applies to your particular appliance.

Cover bowls or casseroles where recommended in recipes

SPEEDY SOUPS AND STARTERS

Satisfying soups and impressive starters can be cooked in next to no time with the aid of the microwave. Whether you want to make a sensational first impression with a luxurious seafood soup, please the family with a creamy chowder or pot a pâté for a party, you'll find plenty of inspiration in this chapter.

Celebration Seafood Soup

375g (12oz) cod or haddock fillets, skinned

2 tblspn olive oil

1 onion, finely chopped

1 green pepper, seeded and chopped

2 cloves garlic, crushed

3 tomatoes, skinned, seeded and roughly chopped

250g (8oz) button mushrooms, halved

300ml (10fl oz) hot chicken or fish stock

125ml (4fl oz) dry white wine

½ tspn dried thyme

generous pinch each dried fennel, powdered saffron and cayenne pepper

2 bay leaves

1 x 250g (8oz) frozen lobster tail, thawed

375g (12oz) cooked crab legs

12 small hard-shell clams, scrubbed

250g (8oz) scallops, rinsed and deveined

375g (12oz) cooked king prawns, peeled and deveined, tails intact

1 Cut the cod or haddock into 2.5cm (1in) cubes. Set aside. Pour the olive oil into the largest casserole that will fit comfortably in your microwave. Stir in the onion, green pepper and garlic. Cover and microwave on High for 3-4 minutes or until the onion is soft, stirring the mixture once.

2 Add the tomatoes, mushrooms, stock and wine to the casserole. Stir in the herbs and spices, including the bay leaves.

3 Replace the cover on the casserole and microwave on High for 5 minutes, then reduce the power to Medium-High and microwave for 10-12 minutes more, or until the flavours are blended, stirring four times.

4 Using kitchen scissors or a sharp knife, cut the lobster shell in half lengthwise, cutting through the meat. Cut the crab legs into 7.5-10cm (3-4in) pieces. Add the lobster, crab legs, clams and scallops to the casserole.

5 Stir the seafood mixture lightly, replace the cover on the casserole and microwave on Medium-High for 15-17 minutes or until the clams begin to open and the scallops are opaque, stirring twice. Discard any clams that fail to open.

6 Add the prawns, replace the cover and allow the soup to stand, covered, for 5 minutes.

7 Discard the bay leaves and serve at once, with chunks of French bread, if liked.

Serves 10-12

Kitchen Tip

Use prime fish and shellfish, bought from a reputable supplier. Mussels may be substituted for the clams, if preferred. Scrub and beard them before use, discarding any whose shells are not tightly closed, and any which fail to open after cooking.

Celebration Seafood Soup

Creamy Corn Chowder

6 rindless streaky bacon rashers, cut into 1cm (½in) pieces

1 onion, finely chopped

½ green pepper, seeded and chopped

60g (2oz) flour

1 litre (1¾pt) milk

freshly ground black pepper

1 egg

1 tblspn chopped fresh parsley

1 x 410g (13oz) can cream-style sweetcorn

1 x 375g (12oz) can whole kernel corn, drained

salt

dash paprika

1 Combine the bacon, onion and green pepper in a large casserole. Microwave on High for 3 minutes or until the vegetables are tender.

2 Put the flour in a small bowl. Gradually stir in 250ml (8fl oz) of the milk until smooth. Add to the bacon mixture with pepper to taste. Microwave on High for about 4 minutes or until thick and bubbly, stirring several times. Stir in remaining milk.

3 Beat the egg lightly in a cup, then beat in a little of the milk mixture. Stir the contents of the cup into the casserole, with the parsley and the cream-style and whole kernel corn.

4 Microwave on High for 10 minutes or until slightly thickened, stirring once. Add salt to taste. Serve in heated bowls, sprinkling each portion with paprika.

Serves 6-8

Lemony Chicken and Rice Soup

30g (1oz) butter

3 tblspn flaked almonds

1 carrot, grated

1 tblspn finely chopped spring onion

1 tblspn chopped fresh parsley

1 tblspn flour

1 x 470g (15oz) can ready-to-serve cream of chicken soup

1 tblspn lemon juice

freshly ground black pepper

2 egg yolks

90g (3oz) cooked chicken, chopped

60g (2oz) cooked long grain rice

1 Put a generous knob of butter in a bowl. Add the almonds and microwave on High for 2-3 minutes or until the almonds are beginning to brown, shaking the bowl once (see Kitchen Tip). Set the almonds aside to cool.

2 Place the remaining butter in a casserole. Add the carrot, spring onion and parsley. Cover and microwave on High for 2-3 minutes or until the carrot is almost tender, stirring once.

3 Stir in the flour, then add the soup and lemon juice, with pepper to taste. Cover and microwave on High for 4-5 minutes, or until the mixture boils.

4 Beat the egg yolks lightly in a cup, then beat in a little of the hot soup mixture. Stir the contents of the cup into the casserole, whisking well. Stir in the chicken and rice. Cover the casserole and microwave on Medium for 1½-2 minutes or until the soup has thickened slightly and the chicken has heated through, stirring twice. Serve in heated bowls, topping each portion with a garnish of browned almonds.

Serves 2

Kitchen Tip
Watch the almonds carefully to avoid the risk of scorching. If preferred, the almonds may be browned in a frying pan on the hob.

Creamy Corn Chowder

Speedy Bacon Soup

1 large carrot, cut in matchsticks

4 sticks celery, thinly sliced

185g (6oz) leeks, trimmed and sliced

315g (10oz) rindless streaky bacon, diced

250g (8oz) Savoy cabbage, shredded

1 litre (1¾pt) chicken stock

125g (4oz) soup pasta shapes

freshly ground black pepper

1 Mix the carrot, celery, leeks and bacon in a large deep casserole. Cover and microwave on High for 10 minutes, stirring the mixture every minute.

2 Add the cabbage, stock and pasta; mix well. Cover and microwave on High for 10-12 minutes or until both vegetables and pasta are tender, stirring three times. Stand for 3 minutes, add pepper to taste and serve.

Serves 4

Speedy Bacon Soup

Chunky Beetroot Soup

2 carrots, thinly sliced

1 large onion, thinly sliced

1 potato, cubed

155g (5oz) cabbage, shredded

1 clove garlic, crushed

1 bay leaf

¼ tspn dried marjoram

600ml (1pt) water

250g (8oz) cooked beetroot, cut into matchsticks

1 x 280g (9oz) can consommé

salt

freshly ground black pepper

soured cream, to serve

1 Combine the vegetables, bay leaf and marjoram in a large deep casserole. Add 125ml (4fl oz) of the measured water. Cover and microwave on High for 12-13 minutes or until tender, stirring the mixture twice.

2 Add the beetroot, remaining water and consommé. Cover and microwave on High for 12-14 minutes or until the beetroot is tender, stirring twice.

3 Remove the bay leaf and add salt and pepper to taste. Serve in heated bowls, topping each portion with soured cream.

Serves 4-6

Cream of Asparagus Soup

30g (1oz) butter

2 sticks celery, finely sliced

1 onion, chopped

500g (1lb) fresh asparagus spears, trimmed, or frozen asparagus, cut into 2.5cm (1in) lengths

600ml (1pt) hot chicken stock

60g (2oz) flour

375ml (12fl oz) milk

salt

freshly ground black pepper

4-6 tblspn single cream

1 Combine the butter, celery and onion in a deep casserole. Microwave on High for 5-7 minutes or until vegetables are tender, stirring once. Add the asparagus and 300ml (10fl oz) of the stock. Cover and microwave for 10 minutes more, stirring once.

2 In a bowl, mix the flour to a paste with a little of the remaining stock, then whisk in the rest of the stock. Add the mixture to the casserole, mixing well. Microwave on High for 2-3 minutes or until thickened, stirring three times.

3 Purée the soup in a blender or food processor, then add the milk and process briefly to mix. Pour the soup into the clean casserole, add salt and pepper to taste and microwave on High for 2-3 minutes until heated through.

4 Serve in heated bowls, swirling 1 tablespoon cream into each portion of soup.

Serves 4-6

Kitchen Tip
Arrange a selection of bread rolls in a napkin-lined wicker basket. Reheat them briefly in the microwave just before serving the soup.

Mediterranean Mussels

2.7kg (6lb) mussels, scrubbed and bearded

5 tblspn dry white wine

1 bouquet garni

3 tblspn olive oil

3 cloves garlic, crushed

2 onions, finely chopped

3 carrots, finely chopped

1 x 397g (13oz) can chopped tomatoes

2 bay leaves

2 tblspn chopped fresh parsley

salt

freshly ground black pepper

1 Divide the mussels into four portions. Put one portion in a large bowl with the wine and bouquet garni. Cover and microwave on High for 5 minutes or until the mussels have opened, stirring once.

2 Lift out the mussels with a slotted spoon, discarding any that remain shut. Use the liquid remaining in the bowl to microwave three more batches in the same way, allowing 4½ minutes each time. When cool enough to handle, remove the mussels from their shells. Strain and reserve the liquid.

3 Place the oil, garlic, onions and carrots in a deep bowl. Microwave on High for 5 minutes or until beginning to soften, stirring twice. Add the tomatoes, reserved liquid from mussels, bay leaves and half the parsley, with salt and pepper to taste. Microwave, uncovered, on High for 6 minutes, stirring the mixture twice.

4 Stir in the mussels. Cover the bowl and microwave on High for 2 minutes or until the mussels are hot and the flavours have blended. Cool, then chill. Remove the bay leaves and serve cold, sprinkled with the remaining parsley.

Serves 8-10

Spanokopetes

½ x 280g (9oz) packet filo pastry (5 sheets)

60g (2oz) butter

Filling

1 x 315g (10oz) packet frozen chopped spinach, thawed

125g (4oz) feta cheese

1 egg, plus 1 egg yolk

2 tblspn double cream

grated nutmeg

salt

freshly ground black pepper

1 Make the filling. Drain the spinach, squeezing out as much liquid as possible. Tip into a bowl and crumble in the feta. Stir in the remaining filling ingredients.

2 Without unfolding the filo sheets, cut them with a pair of scissors into strips 7.5cm (3in) wide. Unroll one strip at a time, covering the remainder with a tea towel to stop them drying out.

3 Brush pastry strip generously with melted butter. Place a heaped teaspoonful of filling on one end of the strip so that the corner can be folded diagonally over it to form a triangle. Keep folding strip over on itself to make a triangular pastry. Repeat with remaining strips and filling.

4 Preheat a large browning dish on High for 5 minutes or according to manufacturer's instructions. Add six pastries; press down. Microwave on High for 1½-2½ minutes, turning once.

5 Remove any cooked pastries after 2 minutes; cool on a wire rack. Cook remaining pastries in the same way, reheating browning dish for 3 minutes when necessary.

Serves 10

Variation
For a deliciously different filling, drain 1 x 425g (13½ oz) can artichoke hearts, chop finely and subtitute for the spinach.

Dolmades

1 x 227g (7oz) packet vine leaves, drained, leaves soaked for 10 minutes in boiling water to cover

lemon wedges to garnish

Filling

2 tblspn olive oil

1 large onion, chopped

1 clove garlic, crushed

1 red pepper, seeded and chopped

185g (6oz) cooked long grain rice

2 tomatoes, skinned, seeded and chopped

8 stoned dates, chopped

30g (1oz) pine nuts, chopped

½ tspn ground allspice

1 Drain the vine leaves and dry on paper towels. Make the filling. Place the oil in a deep bowl with the onion, garlic and red pepper. Microwave on High for 4 minutes or until softened, stirring once. Stir in the remaining filling ingredients and mix well.

2 Divide the filling between the vine leaves, folding the sides over the filling and rolling each leaf up neatly from the stem end. Place join side down in a shallow dish. Cover and microwave on High for 4 minutes, giving the dish a quarter turn every minute, if necessary. Serve at room temperature, with lemon wedges.

Serves 8-10

Hummus

125g (4oz) chick peas, soaked overnight in water to cover

3 cloves garlic, crushed

2 onions, finely chopped

600ml (1pt) boiling water

2 tblspn tahini

4 tblspn Greek yogurt

lemon juice

salt

freshly ground black pepper

1 Drain the chick peas. Put them in a deep bowl with the garlic, onions and boiling water. Cover and microwave on High for 45 minutes or until the chick peas are tender, stirring occasionally. Remove the bowl from the microwave and allow to stand, covered, until the chick peas are cool.

2 Purée the chick pea mixture in a blender or food processor until smooth. Add the tahini and yogurt and process to combine. Scrape the hummus into a bowl, add lemon juice, salt and pepper to taste and serve cold, with vegetable dippers, if liked.

Serves 6

Mediterranean Mussels, Dolmades, Leek Eggah (page 34), Hummus and Spanokopetes, with Taramasalata and Feta cheese

Turkey and Artichoke Salad

Red Bean Pâté

1 small onion, finely chopped

1 clove garlic, crushed

1 green chilli, seeded and finely chopped

2 tblspn oil

1 x 425g (13½ oz) can red kidney beans

1 tspn lemon juice

2 tblspn tomato purée

dash Tabasco sauce

salt

1 Combine the onion, garlic, chilli and oil in a deep bowl. Microwave on High for 4 minutes.

2 Drain the kidney beans, reserving 2 tblspn of the can liquid. Add to the bowl with the lemon juice, tomato purée and Tabasco. Cover and microwave on High for 4 minutes, stirring once.

3 Purée the mixture with the reserved can liquid in a blender or food processor. Add salt to taste. Spoon into 4 ramekins. When cool, cover and chill. Serve with toast.

Serves 4

Turkey and Artichoke Salad

1 onion, finely chopped

1 clove garlic, crushed

¼ tspn dried sage

pinch dried thyme

250g (8oz) turkey breast steak, cut into 2.5cm (1in) cubes

1 x 425g (13½oz) can artichoke hearts, drained, artichokes halved

1 x 425g (13½oz) can cannellini beans, drained

1 small red pepper, seeded and chopped

1 tblspn chopped fresh parsley

Dressing

3 tblspn sunflower oil

2 tblspn white wine vinegar

dash Tabasco sauce

salt

1 Place the onion, garlic and herbs in a deep bowl. Cover and microwave on High for 1-1½ minutes or until the onion is beginning to soften.

2 Stir in the turkey cubes and halved artichoke halves. Replace the cover and microwave on High for 5-8 minutes, or until the turkey is no longer pink, stirring the mixture twice.

3 Using a slotted spoon, transfer the turkey and artichokes with the onion and herbs to a salad bowl. Add the beans, red pepper and parsley; mix lightly but well.

4 Make the dressing by shaking the oil, vinegar and Tabasco, with salt to taste, in a tightly closed screw top jar. Pour over the salad; toss to coat. When cool, cover and refrigerate for 3 hours. Serve on individual plates, garnished with endive, if liked.

Serves 6

Smoked Salmon Pâté

60g (2oz) butter

250g (8oz) smoked salmon trimmings

2 tblspn mayonnaise

2 tblspn crème fraîche

3 tblspn lemon juice

salt

freshly ground black pepper

Garnish

lemon twists

parsley sprigs

1 Place the butter in a small bowl, cover and microwave on Medium for 30-45 seconds or until soft, but not melted.

2 Combine the softened butter, salmon trimmings, mayonnaise, crème fraîche and lemon juice in a blender or food processor. Add salt and pepper to taste. Purée until smooth.

3 Divide the mixture between 6 small ramekins. Cover and chill until firm. Garnish with lemon twists and parsley. Serve with Melba toast, if liked.

Serves 6

Hot Avocado and Prawns

3 ripe avocados

4 tspn lemon juice

2 tspn sunflower oil

4 spring onions, chopped

185 g/6 oz peeled cooked prawns

3 tblspn natural low fat yogurt

½ tspn creamed horseradish

3 tblspn mayonnaise

salt

freshly ground black pepper

Garnish

8 whole cooked prawns

snipped chives

1 Cut the avocados in half lengthwise, remove the stones and scoop out the flesh, taking care not to damage the shells. Brush the inside of each avocado shell with a little of the lemon juice, wrap closely in clingfilm and set aside.

2 Cut the avocado flesh into small cubes, place in a bowl and toss with the remaining lemon juice.

3 Combine the oil and spring onions in a deep bowl, cover and microwave on High for 1½ minutes or until the onion is softened, stirring twice. Add the prawns, turning them gently until coated in the flavoured oil. Replace the cover and microwave on High for 2 minutes or until the prawns are heated through.

4 Stir the cubed avocado and lemon juice into the prawn mixture; mix gently to coat.

5 Fold the yogurt into the mixture. Stir the horseradish into the mayonnaise until thoroughly mixed, then add to the bowl and fold in gently. Add salt and pepper to taste.

6 Unwrap the avocado shells and divide the mixture between them. Arrange the filled shells on a large plate with the pointed ends towards the centre. Microwave on High for 2-2½ minutes or until heated through.

7 Garnish with the whole prawns and snipped chives. Serve at once with bread and butter.

Serves 4

Kitchen Tip
To remove the stone cleanly from an avocado, strike it firmly and decisively with the blade of a broad, non-serrated knife. When the knife is lifted, the stone will come away too. Should it leave a brown husk behind, simply lift this out with a spoon.

Hot Avocado and Prawns

FAST FISH

One of the microwave's most notable success stories is the cooking of fish. Thanks to the texture and moisture content, fish and shellfish cook rapidly to tender perfection – so rapidly, in fact, that it is vital to check fish frequently to avoid overcooking.

Paella

2 tblspn olive oil

1 large onion, chopped

2 cloves garlic, crushed

500g (1lb) long grain rice

850ml (1pt 8fl oz) boiling chicken stock

4 pinches saffron threads

185g (6oz) frozen peas

250g (8oz) mussels, scrubbed and bearded

60ml (¼ cup) dry white wine

16 cooked prawns

15g (½oz) butter, melted

½ tspn paprika

4 chicken thighs

500g (1lb) chorizo sausages, sliced

2 tomatoes, skinned, seeded and quartered

1 Place oil, chopped onion and crushed garlic in a large deep bowl. Cover and microwave on High for 4 minutes or until softened.

2 Stir in rice, boiling stock and saffron threads. Cover with vented microwave stretch film and microwave on High for 5 minutes, then on Medium for 10-12 minutes or until liquid is absorbed, stirring the rice twice.

3 Stir in frozen peas, cover bowl and set aside.

4 Place the prepared mussels in a deep bowl with the wine. Cover with vented microwave stretch film.

5 Microwave on High for 1-2 minutes or until the mussels have opened. Discard any that remain shut.

6 Using a slotted spoon, add mussels to rice mixture. Stir in prawns, replace the cover and set the bowl aside.

7 Mix the melted butter and paprika in a small bowl. Brush over chicken thighs. Microwave on a roasting rack on High for 10-15 minutes or until chicken is no longer pink, rearranging once.

8 Add the sliced chorizo to the rice mixture with the chicken and tomatoes. Mix lightly. Cover bowl and microwave on High for 5 minutes. Serve at once, with crusty bread and a green salad.

Serves 4

Variations
The ingredients for paella can be varied according to what is available and to suit the tastes of your guests. Clams may be substituted for the mussels, and sliced scallops make an excellent addition. Use cubed ham instead of chorizo, if preferred. If fresh or frozen mussels are difficult to come by, use smoked mussels, adding them 2 minutes before the end of the final cooking time.

Paella

Trout with Mushroom Stuffing

4 x 250g (8oz) frozen trout

orange slices, to garnish

Stuffing

375g (12oz) button mushrooms

½ small red pepper, seeded and finely chopped

2 sticks celery, finely chopped

1 tblspn corn oil

60g (2oz) ground almonds

3 tblspn fresh white or wholemeal breadcrumbs

1 tblspn chopped fresh parsley

2 tblspn orange juice

salt

freshly ground black pepper

Topping

60g (2oz) flaked almonds

60g (2oz) butter

1 Place the trout in a shallow dish, cover with paper towels and microwave on Defrost for 19-21 minutes or until softened but still cold, turning over several times. Stand for 5 minutes, then rinse cavities with cold water until no longer icy, if necessary.

2 Make the stuffing. Place the mushrooms in a dish, cover with paper towels and microwave on High for 2½-3 minutes or until softened. Drain well, pat dry and chop finely.

3 Place the red pepper, celery and oil in a bowl. Cover and microwave on High for 4 minutes or until the vegetables are tender, stirring twice. Stir in mushrooms and remaining stuffing ingredients. Cool the stuffing slightly.

4 Skin the trout, if liked. Divide the stuffing between the cavities, then arrange the fish in a shallow buttered dish.

5 Make the topping by microwaving the almonds with the butter in a bowl on High for 2 minutes, shaking the bowl several times. Watch the nuts carefully; do not allow them to scorch.

6 Spoon the almond mixture over the trout, cover and microwave on High for 7-9 minutes or until the flesh flakes easily when tested with the tip of a knife. Stand for 5 minutes, then serve.

Serves 4

Malay Prawn Casserole

250g (8oz) green beans, sliced

2 tblspn water

2 large onions, chopped

45g (1½oz) butter

1 red pepper, seeded and cut into small strips

90g (3oz) mushrooms, sliced

3 tblspn Malaysian mild curry paste

2 tblspn tomato purée

125g (4oz) creamed coconut

155ml (5fl oz) boiling milk

410g (13oz) peeled cooked prawns, thawed if frozen

1 Put the beans in a bowl with the measured water. Cover and cook on High for 6 minutes; drain and set aside.

2 Place the onions and butter in a deep casserole. Cover and microwave on High for 5 minutes or until softened, stirring twice.

3 Add pepper strips, replace the cover and microwave on High for 3 minutes. Stir in mushrooms, curry paste and tomato purée. Cook for 3 minutes more or until vegetables are very tender, stirring mixture twice.

4 Place the creamed coconut in a bowl. Stir in the boiling milk and microwave on High for 2-3 minutes, stirring once during cooking and again when cooking is complete, until smooth.

5 Stir coconut milk into mixture, then add prawns and beans; mix lightly. Cover and microwave on High for 4 minutes or until prawns are hot, stirring twice.

Serves 4-6

Siena Sole

4 x 250g (8oz) lemon sole or Dover sole fillets, skinned

paprika, for dusting

Stuffing

185g (6oz) cream cheese

250g (8oz) frozen chopped spinach, thawed

4 tblspn fresh white breadcrumbs

2 tblspn finely chopped pecan nuts

2 tspn milk

2 tspn mayonnaise

salt

1 Cut each fillet into 4 even pieces. Cut long slits in 4 of the pieces for the stuffing. Place the cut pieces on top of the uncut fish and place in a large buttered dish.

2 Place the cream cheese in a bowl and microwave on Medium for 25-30 seconds until soft. Stir in the remaining stuffing ingredients.

Salmon Steaks with Dill Sauce

Mackerel with Courgette and Horseradish Stuffing

2 x 500g (1lb) mackerel, cleaned

Stuffing

3 spring onions, chopped

1 tblspn corn oil

2 tblspn long grain rice

155ml (5fl oz) water

freshly ground black pepper

2 courgettes, grated

½ small red pepper, seeded and finely chopped

2 tblspn creamed horseradish

salt

1 Make the stuffing. Combine the spring onions and oil in a deep bowl, cover and microwave on High for 2 minutes or until the spring onions are tender.

2 Add the rice and measured water, with pepper to taste. Replace the cover and microwave on High for 12 minutes, or until nearly all the water has been absorbed, stirring twice.

3 Stir in the courgettes, red pepper and horseradish. Cover bowl and microwave on High for 3 minutes. Add salt to taste.

4 Spoon half the stuffing into each mackerel cavity; wrap each fish in microwave stretch wrap or place in a roasting bag. Pierce the wrap or seal the bag loosely to allow the steam to escape. Microwave on Medium for 7 minutes or until the fish flesh flakes easily when tested with the tip of a knife. Turn the fish over halfway through cooking.

5 Stand for 5 minutes, then cut open the wrap or bag, transfer the fish to individual plates and serve at once.

Serves 2

Kitchen Tip
When choosing mackerel, look for fish with bright eyes, red gills and clear skin markings.

---

3 Open the slits on the cut fish to form pockets; stuff with the cream cheese and spinach mixture. Dust with a little paprika and cover with buttered greaseproof paper.

4 Microwave on Medium for 10-11 minutes or until the fish flesh flakes when tested with the tip of a knife, turning dish twice during cooking. Stand for 5 minutes. Serve.

Serves 4

Salmon Steaks in Dill Sauce

4 x 185g (6oz) salmon steaks

Sauce

60g (2oz) butter

4 tblspn lemon juice

1 tblspn whole sesame seeds

¼ tspn sugar

1 clove garlic, crushed

2 tblspn chopped dill

1 Combine all ingredients for the sauce in a measuring jug. Microwave on High for 1½ minutes until the butter has melted and the sauce is hot, stirring once.

2 Arrange the salmon steaks in a shallow dish, with the thinner tails towards the centre. Brush them with a little of the sauce. Cover with greaseproof paper and microwave on Medium for about 10 minutes, until the fish is almost cooked, rearranging the steaks after 6 minutes. Leave the fish to stand for 4 minutes.

3 Reheat the remaining sauce on High for 1 minute. Meanwhile arrange the salmon steaks on a serving platter. Stir the sauce, pour it over the fish and serve. Parsley sprigs and lemon wedges may be used as a garnish, or the salmon may be served with grilled cherry tomatoes and sprigs of dill.

Serves 4

Shrimp Creole

2 sticks celery, chopped

½ green pepper, diced

1 small onion, finely chopped

1 clove garlic, crushed

1 tblspn olive oil

2 x 397g (13oz) cans chopped tomatoes with herbs

2 tblspn flour

1 tspn lemon juice

¼ tspn cayenne pepper

375g (12oz) uncooked king prawns, peeled and deveined, tails intact

salt

freshly ground black pepper

4-6 portions cooked long grain rice, to serve

1 Combine the vegetables and olive oil in a deep casserole. Cover and microwave on High for 3-5 minutes until the vegetables are tender.

2 Drain the canned tomatoes, reserving the juice in a measuring jug. Whisk the flour into the juice until smooth. Add the mixture to the vegetables with the chopped tomatoes, lemon juice and cayenne. Cover with vented microwave stretch wrap. Microwave on High for 7-8 minutes, stirring mixture twice.

3 Stir in the prawns, with salt and pepper to taste. Replace the cover, reduce power to Medium and microwave for 10-15 minutes or until the prawns are opaque, stirring several times.

4 Reheat the rice in the microwave. Arrange on a platter, pour over the shrimp mixture and serve.

Serves 4-6

Golden Kedgeree

In Victorian times, kedgeree was traditionally served as part of the formal breakfast buffet, and it is still to be found alongside the scrambled eggs and devilled kidneys in some establishments. Kedgeree makes an excellent supper dish too.

½ onion, finely chopped

1 red pepper, seeded and chopped

pinch of saffron powder

125g (4oz) frozen peas

25g (1oz) butter

90g (3oz) long grain white rice

90g (3oz) long grain brown rice

470ml (15fl oz) boiling chicken or fish stock

500g (1lb) smoked cod or haddock fillet, skinned and boned, cut into even chunks

parsley sprig to garnish

1 Combine the onion, red pepper, saffron, peas, butter, both types of rice and the boiling stock in a large deep bowl. Cover with microwave stretch wrap. Pierce the wrap in several places, or lift one corner to allow steam to escape. Microwave the mixture on High for 16-18 minutes, stirring twice.

2 Arrange the chunks of smoked cod or haddock in a layer over the rice mixture. Replace the cover and microwave on High for 6-7 minutes until the fish is cooked. Gently stir it into the rice.

3 Stand, covered, for 3 minutes, then tip onto a serving platter. Garnish with parsley and serve.

Serves 4-6

Kitchen Tip
Serve the kedgeree with low fat natural yogurt and wedges of hard-boiled egg, if liked.

Monkfish Stew

25g (1oz) butter

1 onion, thinly sliced

1 x 397g (13oz) can chopped tomatoes

1 large green pepper, seeded and sliced

1 clove garlic, crushed

185ml (6fl oz) hot fish stock

375g (12oz) monkfish tail fillet or gemfish, cut into bite-size pieces

60g (2oz) peeled cooked prawns

1 x 315g (10oz) can clams in brine, rinsed and drained

2 courgettes, cut in matchsticks

½ tspn grated nutmeg

salt

freshly ground black pepper

1 tblspn cornflour

2 tblspn water

chopped fresh parsley, to garnish

1 Place the butter and onion in a deep casserole, cover and microwave on High for 2 minutes or until the onion is soft.

2 Add the tomatoes, green pepper, garlic, stock, fish, prawns, clams, courgettes and nutmeg, with salt and pepper to taste. Mix well.

3 Cover and microwave on High for 5 minutes, stirring once. Reduce the power to Medium-High and cook for 20 minutes or until the flesh of the fish flakes easily when tested with the tip of a knife. Stir twice during cooking.

4 Mix the cornflour with the measured water in a cup. Stir the mixture into the casserole, mixing well. Microwave on High for 2-3 minutes to thicken the stew, stirring once during cooking and again when cooking is complete. Sprinkle with parsley and serve, with foccacia or a similar country-style bread, if liked.

Serves 4

Duck with Green Olives

4 x 375g (12oz) duck quarters

1 onion, chopped

300ml (10fl oz) dry white wine

1 tblspn tomato purée

½ tspn dried thyme

½ tspn dried rosemary

1 bay leaf

freshly ground black pepper

250g (8oz) button mushrooms, halved

375g (12oz) stoned green olives

1 Wipe the duck with paper towels. Using a sharp knife, make diagonal cuts in the skin to form diamond patterns.

2 Place the chopped onion in a deep casserole which is large enough to hold all the duck portions in a single layer (while still fitting in your microwave). Moisten the onion with 2 tablespoons of the wine.

3 Micowave the onion mixture on High for 2-3 minutes or until tender. Stir in the remaining wine, tomato purée and herbs, with pepper to taste. Arrange the duck on top of the onion mixture, cover and microwave on High for 15 minutes, rearranging the duck once. Add the mushrooms and olives. Replace the cover, reduce the power to Medium and microwave for 30 minutes or until the duck is tender and the juices run clear, rearranging once.

4 Transfer the duck portions to a grill pan and place under a preheated hot grill for 3-5 minutes or until golden brown.

5 Meanwhile, skim the fat from the sauce remaining in the casserole. Remove the bay leaf. Microwave on High for 3 minutes. Serve the duck on a serving platter with the mushrooms and olives. Offer the sauce separately.

Serves 4

Moroccan Chicken

3 carrots, thinly sliced

1 large onion, chopped

250g (8oz) swede, diced

1 tspn ground coriander

½ tspn ground cinnamon

¼ tspn cayenne pepper

½ tspn caraway seeds

2 courgettes, sliced

1 x 397g (13oz) can chopped tomatoes

2 tblspn tomato purée

60g (2oz) raisins

4 chicken breasts on the bone, skinned

salt

freshly ground black pepper

1 Place carrots, onion, swede and spices in a large casserole. Cover and microwave on High for 12 minutes or until vegetables are tender, stirring twice.

2 Stir in the courgettes, tomatoes, tomato purée and raisins. Arrange the chicken breasts on top.

3 Cover and microwave on High for 20 minutes or until the meat near the bone is no longer pink. Rearrange chicken and stir vegetables once. Add salt and pepper to taste. Stand for 5 minutes before serving the chicken.

Serves 4

Goulash

450g (1lb) lean braising steak, cut into 1 cm (½in) cubes

2 onions, thinly sliced

2 red peppers, seeded and thinly sliced

2 x 397g (13oz) cans chopped tomatoes

6 tblspn tomato purée

2 tblspn mild paprika

salt

freshly ground black pepper

155ml (5fl oz) soured cream

Duck with Green Olives

Bacon-wrapped Mini Meatloaves

1 Place the steak in a casserole with the onions, red peppers, tomatoes, tomato purée and paprika. Stir well to mix. Cover and microwave on High for 6-8 minutes.

2 Stir the steak mixture well, reduce the power to Medium and microwave for 30-40 minutes more or until the meat is tender, stirring occasionally.

3 Stand, covered, for 5 minutes, then add salt and pepper to taste. Spoon a generous dollop of soured cream on top of each portion when serving. Add a dusting of paprika, if liked.

Serves 4

Kitchen Tip
Veal may be used instead of braising steak. It will require less time to become tender.
Alternatively, break with tradition and use diced turkey.

Bacon-wrapped Mini Meatloaves

8 rindless streaky bacon rashers

½ green pepper, seeded and finely chopped

1 small onion, finely chopped

1 tblspn corn oil

500g (1lb) lean minced beef

45g (1½oz) fresh white breadcrumbs

2 tblspn milk

1 egg, beaten

2 tblspn tomato ketchup

2 tblspn Worcestershire sauce

1 tblspn ground coriander

1 tspn ground cumin

1 Put the bacon between 4 double thickness sheets of paper towel. Microwave on High for 3 minutes only (so that the bacon remains slightly underdone). Set aside.

2 Put the green pepper and onion in a bowl with the oil. Cover and microwave for 3-4 minutes or until just tender. Add the remaining ingredients and mix thoroughly, using a wooden spoon.

3 Divide the mixture in half and shape each portion into a 15 x 9cm (6 x 3½in) loaf. Wrap 4 bacon rashers around each loaf and secure with wooden cocktail sticks.

4 Place the loaves on a microwave roasting rack, cover with a double thickness of paper towels and microwave on High for 10 minutes. If you do not have a turntable, give the roasting rack a quarter turn twice during cooking.

5 Cover with foil (shiny side in) and leave to stand for 5 minutes before serving.

Serves 4

SIDELINES

True colours, crisp-tender textures and pure flavours are just some of the advantages associated with cooking vegetables in the microwave. Jacket potatoes are the best documented success story, but most vegetables benefit dramatically from this form of cooking. In most cases only a very small amount of liquid is required.

Cabbage in Cheese Sauce

750g (1½lb) Savoy cabbage

4 tblspn water

Cheese Sauce

30g (1oz) butter, cubed

2 tblspn flour

300ml (10fl oz) milk

125g (4oz) Cheddar Cheese, grated

salt

freshly ground black pepper

1 Trim and quarter the cabbage. Cut away and discard the central core. Arrange the cabbage quarters like wheel spokes in a large shallow casserole.

2 Add the measured water, cover the casserole and microwave on High for 10-12 minutes or until the cabbage is tender, turning dish once during cooking. Stand, covered, for 5 minutes.

3 Make the sauce. Melt the butter in a measuring jug on High for 15-30 seconds. Stir in the flour, then blend in the milk. Microwave for 3-4 minutes on High until the sauce is smooth and thick, stirring several times. Stir in half the cheese, with salt and pepper to taste.

4 Drain the cabbage. Pour the cheese sauce over the top and sprinkle with the remaining cheese. Microwave on High for 45-60 seconds until the cheese topping has melted.

Serves 4

Cabbage in Cheese Sauce

Carrot Curls

2 large carrots

2 tblspn water

60g (2oz) butter, cubed

½ tspn caster sugar

salt

1 Using a vegetable peeler, shave the carrots lengthwise to produce curls. Place in a large bowl with the measured water, butter and sugar. Cover and microwave on High for 3-4 minutes, stirring once.

2 Drain off most of the liquid, add salt to taste and toss lightly. Serve at once.

Serves 4

Green Beans and Broccoli

750g (1½lb) broccoli, cut into even-sized florets

250g (8oz) whole green beans

2 tblspn water

salt

freshly ground black pepper

30g (1oz) butter

1 Combine the broccoli and beans in a large casserole. Add the measured water, cover and microwave on High for 10-13 minutes, stirring halfway through cooking.

2 Add salt and pepper to taste. Dot with butter, replace the cover and allow to stand for 5 minutes before tossing lightly and serving.

Serves 6

Cauliflower and Mushroom Medley

1 onion, chopped

2 tblspn water

500g (1lb) cauliflower florets

1 tblspn chopped fresh parsley

1 tspn chopped fresh thyme

125g (4oz) mushrooms, sliced

150ml (5fl oz) natural low fat yogurt

freshly ground black pepper

1 Place onion and measured water in a large bowl or casserole. Cover and microwave on High for 1 minute.

2 Stir in cauliflower, parsley and thyme. Replace cover and microwave on High for 6-7 minutes or until cauliflower is crisp-tender.

3 Stir in mushrooms, replace cover and microwave on High for 3 minutes, stirring once.

4 Make the sauce. Mix the yogurt and pepper in a small bowl. Microwave on Medium for 30-60 seconds, until hot but not boiling. Drain the vegetables, pour over the sauce and serve.

Serves 4

Wine-braised Celery

2 heads of celery, trimmed

30g (1oz) butter

125g (4oz) rindless back bacon, cut into strips

½ onion, chopped

2 tspn cornflour

250ml (8fl oz) white wine

150ml (5fl oz) hot beef stock

1 Cut the whole heads of celery in half lengthwise, then trim to fit an oval or rectangular dish which can be accommodated in your microwave. Arrange the celery in a single layer in the dish and pour in cold water to cover.

2 Cover the dish and microwave on High for 7-8 minutes or until the celery is crisp-tender. Drain off the water and set the dish aside.

3 Combine the butter, bacon and onion in a bowl. Cover and microwave on High for 2-5 minutes or until onion is softened. Stir in the cornflour, then the wine and stock.

4 Pour the mixture over the celery, cover and microwave on High for 8-10 minutes or until the celery hearts are very tender. Stand, covered, for 5 minutes. Serve.

Serves 4

Variation

Use 1 sliced leek instead of the onion, if preferred, and substitute chicken stock for the beef stock.

Jacket Potato

Jacket Potatoes

4 large baking potatoes, about 375g (12oz) each

butter, soured cream or Greek yogurt to serve

1 Scrub the potatoes well, prick them with a fork to prevent them from bursting during cooking, and arrange them in a circle on a paper towel in the microwave.

2 Microwave on High for 20-22 minutes or until the potatoes are soft and yielding when gently squeezed. Turn the potatoes over halfway through cooking.

3 Transfer the potatoes to a serving platter, cut a cross in the top of each, and squeeze the opposite sides of each potato to reveal the fluffy cooked centre. Take care as the potatoes will be very hot.

4 Serve at once, with butter, soured cream or Greek yogurt. Alternatively, try one of the fillings listed below.

Serves 4

Fillings

As soon as the potatoes are cool enough to handle, cut them in half and scoop the flesh into a bowl. Mash the potato with the filling ingredients, pile it back into the potato shells, arrange around the rim of a plate and microwave on High for 1-2 minutes to heat.

Cheese: Mash the cooked potato with 45g (1½oz) butter. Stir in 90g (3oz) grated Cheddar, Red Leicester or Gruyère cheese. Return the flavoured potato to the shells, top with more grated cheese if liked, and reheat.

Bacon and Sweetcorn: Dice 3 rindless streaky bacon rashers. Cook on High for 2 minutes, then drain on paper towels. Mash the cooked potato with 45g (1½oz) butter. Stir in 125g (4oz) creamed sweetcorn, with the crispy bacon bits. Fill shells and reheat.

Sausage and Pimiento: Mash the cooked potato with 45g (1½oz) butter. Stir in 4 sliced grilled chipolatas and 4 tablespoons chopped canned pimiento. Fill shells and reheat.

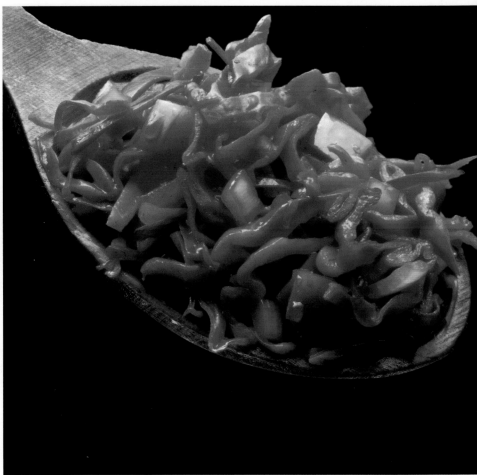

Spiced Red Cabbage

Rosemary Potatoes

4 medium baking potatoes

2 tablespoons olive oil

rosemary sprigs

rock salt

freshly ground black pepper

1 Scrub the potatoes, prick them with a fork, and place on a paper towel in the microwave.

2 Microwave on High for about 15 minutes until just tender. Turn the potatoes over half way through cooking.

3 When the potatoes are cool enough to handle, chop into large cubes.

4 Arrange the potatoes in a single layer in an ovenproof dish, drizzle with olive oil and add the rosemary sprigs. Place under a preheated hot grill for 3-4 minutes until golden. Add salt and pepper to serve.

Serves 4

Spiced Red Cabbage

2 tblspn unsweetened apple juice

1 tblspn soft light brown sugar

2 tspn cider vinegar

¼ tspn ground cinnamon

pinch ground cloves

500g (1lb) red cabbage, trimmed and finely shredded

1 cooking apple, peeled and diced

1 onion, finely chopped

15g (½oz) butter, diced

salt

freshly ground black pepper

1 Combine all the ingredients except the seasoning in a deep casserole. Mix well. Cover and microwave on High for 8-10 minutes, stirring twice.

2 Let stand, covered, for 5 minutes. Stir in seasoning to taste, then serve.

Serves 4

Cheesy Bacon Toast

Cheesy Bacon Toast

6 rindless streaky bacon rashers

4 slices white bread

2 tomatoes, sliced

4 slices processed cheese, each slice cut in half diagonally

1 Place the bacon on a double thickness of paper towel and cover with two more layers. Microwave on High for 3-3½ minutes or until bacon is almost cooked. Allow to stand for 5 minutes.

2 Toast the bread, then arrange tomato slices on each slice. Cut the bacon rashers in half and place three pieces of bacon on each slice of toast. Overlap the cheese triangles on top.

3 Place two of the bacon topped toasts on paper towels. Microwave on High for 30-60 seconds or until the cheese melts. Repeat with the remaining toasts.

Serves 2-4

Mixed Cheese Fondue

4 tspn cornflour

300ml (10fl oz) dry white wine

125g (4oz) Emmental cheese, grated

185g (6oz) Gruyère cheese, grated

1 tblspn kirsch

grated nutmeg, see method

white pepper

bread cubes to serve

1 In a deep casserole, blend the cornflour to a paste with a little of the wine. Stir in the remaining wine and microwave on High for 4-5 minutes, stirring every 30 seconds.

2 Stir the cheeses into the wine until melted, then add the kirsch, with nutmeg and white pepper to taste.

3 Microwave on Low for 1-2 minutes, stirring every 15 seconds. Serve with bread cubes speared on fondue forks.

Serves 4

Hot Baps Italiennes

4 baps or large soft bread rolls

45g (1½oz) butter, softened

125g (4oz) mozzarella cheese

2 tomatoes

2 tspn chopped fresh oregano

salt

freshly ground black pepper

watercress sprigs, black olives and anchovies, to serve

1 Make four parallel slits in the top of each bap or roll, cutting almost but not quite through to the base. Butter the bread on either side of each slit.

2 Cut the mozzarella into eight slices and place a slice in the central two slits in each bap. Slice each tomato into four and sprinkle with the oregano, salt and pepper. Place a slice in the outer slits in each bap.

3 Arrange the baps in a ring on paper towels; microwave on High for 2½ minutes or until the cheese starts to melt. Serve garnished with watercress, olives and anchovies.

Serves 4

Tuna Muffins

1 x 220g (7oz) can tuna, drained

2 hard-boiled eggs, chopped

3 tblspn mayonnaise

½ onion, finely chopped

2 tblspn cucumber relish

2 tblspn stuffed olives or capers

½ tspn made mustard

salt

freshly ground black pepper

4 muffins, split

2 beefsteak tomatoes, sliced

60g (2oz) Cheddar cheese, grated

1 Combine the tuna, eggs, mayonnaise, onion, relish, olives or capers and mustard in a bowl. Add salt and pepper to taste; mix well. Divide the mixture between the muffin halves. Top each muffin half with a slice of tomato and a little of the grated Cheddar cheese.

2 Place four muffin halves on a large plate lined with two paper towels. Microwave on High for 2-3 minutes or until the cheese melts, rotating once if necessary. Repeat with remaining muffins.

Serves 4

Salami Torpedo

---
1 small French stick

30-45g (1-1½ oz) garlic butter

25g (1oz) salami slices, halved
---
2 large tomatoes, sliced
---

1 Cut the bread vertically in 2.5cm (1in) slices, cutting almost, but not quite through to the base.

2 Spread the butter over both sides of the slices and place 1 salami and 1 tomato slice in each slit. Re-form the loaf neatly, wrap it in greaseproof paper and dampen the paper lightly.

3 Microwave on High for 1-1½ minutes or until the butter has melted and the bread is warm. Unwrap and serve at once.

Serves 2

Seafood Casserole

---
2 tblspn flour
---
pinch dry mustard

250ml (8fl oz) milk

30g (1oz) butter, cubed
---
salt
---
freshly ground black pepper

60g (2oz) Cheddar cheese, grated
---
1 x 200g (6½oz) can tuna, drained and flaked

110g (3½oz) can prawns, drained

185g (6oz) mushrooms, sliced
---
1 stick celery, thinly sliced
---
1 small onion, chopped

½ green pepper, cut in thin strips
---
2 tblspn water

90g (3oz) canned chow mein noodles or potato sticks
---

1 Combine the flour and mustard in a deep bowl. Gradually whisk in the milk, then add the butter, with salt and pepper to taste. Microwave on High for 4-5 minutes, whisking twice during cooking, until thickened and smooth. Whisk in the cheese until melted, then stir in the drained tuna, prawns and mushrooms. Set aside.

2 Place the celery, onion and green pepper in a deep casserole. Add the measured water. Microwave on High for 3 minutes or until softened, stirring twice. Drain off the liquid.

3 Stir in the cheese sauce mixture. Microwave on High for 2 minutes. Stir in two thirds of the noodles or potato sticks; sprinkle the remainder on top. Serve the casserole at once.

Serves 4

Seafood Casserole

HEY PRESTO PUDDINGS

Now you see them – now you don't! Dish up delicious desserts made in your microwave and watch them vanish before your eyes!

Fresh Fruit Flapjack

140g (4½oz) butter

125g (4oz) soft light brown sugar

185g (6oz) porridge oats

60g (2oz) walnuts or pecan nuts, chopped

Topping

125g (4oz) large strawberries, hulled and sliced

125g (4oz) black grapes, halved and seeded

1 x 470g (15oz) can apricots in fruit juice, drained, juice reserved

2 kiwi fruit, peeled, halved and sliced

2 tspn cornflour

1 tspn lemon juice

1 Place the butter in a deep bowl, cover and microwave on High for 1-1½ minutes or until melted. Stir in the sugar, oats and nuts.

2 Pat the mixture firmly over the base of a 25cm (10in) flat platter. Microwave on High for 4 minutes, giving a quarter turn once if necessary, until almost set. Cool.

3 Arrange the strawberry slices in a thick overlapping band across the centre of the cooled flapjack base. Microwave, uncovered, on High for 15-30 seconds, until the fruit is just warm.

4 Place a row of grapes on either side of the strawberry slices. Microwave on High for 15-30 seconds, then place a row of apricots on either side of the grapes and microwave on High for 15-30 seconds more.

5 Complete the covering of the flapjack base by adding overlapping slices of kiwi fruit on either side of the apricots. Microwave on High for 15-30 seconds.

6 In a measuring jug, mix 3 tablespoons of the reserved fruit juice with the cornflour and lemon juice until smooth. Cover and microwave on High for 3-4 minutes, stirring twice, until thick and glossy. Spoon over the fruit. Serve the flapjack warm or cold.

Serves 6

Orange-glazed Pears

2 Williams pears, halved and cored

3 tablespoons orange liqueur

1 tablespoon sultanas

grated rind of 1 orange

1 tspn cornflour

3 tblspn water

pinch of ground allspice

pinch of ground cinnamon

1 Arrange the pears, cut side up, in a baking dish, with the narrower ends pointing to the centre of the dish.

2 Combine the orange liqueur, sultanas, orange rind, cornflour, water and spices in a measuring jug. Mix until smooth. Microwave on High for 1-2 minutes or until thickened, stirring twice.

3 Pour the mixture over the pears. Cover and microwave on High for 3-5 minutes or until the pears are tender, rearranging and basting once. Stand, covered, for 5 minutes.

4 Transfer the pears to individual serving dishes and pour a little of the hot syrup over each. Serve at once.

Serves 2-4

Fresh Fruit Flapjack

Savoury Cheese Bread

Savoury Cheese Bread

250g (8oz) plain flour

1 tblspn grated onion

2 tspn poppy seeds

2 tspn sugar

1½ tspn baking powder

½ tspn bicarbonate of soda

½ tspn salt

60g (2oz) Cheddar cheese, grated

75g (2½oz) butter or margarine

125ml (4fl oz) buttermilk or soured milk

1 egg, lightly beaten

Topping

1 tspn melted butter

2 tblspn dry breadcrumbs

2 tblspn grated Parmesan cheese

1 tspn poppy seeds

1 Combine the flour, grated onion, poppy seeds, sugar, baking powder, bicarbonate of soda, salt and grated cheese in a large bowl. Cut in the butter and rub in until well distributed. Alternatively, prepare the mixture in a food processor, using the steel blade and processing for just long enough to break down the butter. Add the buttermilk and egg and mix quickly to a soft dough.

2 Lightly grease a 25cm (10in) pie dish or round baking dish; base line with nonstick baking paper. Shape the dough into a round and place in the dish.

3 Mix the topping ingredients and sprinkle over the dough round, then use a sharp knife to score the surface in a neat criss-cross pattern.

4 Microwave on Medium for 6 minutes, then increase power to High and microwave for 3-5 minutes more until firm in the centre. Stand for 10 minutes. Serve warm or cold, in wedges.

Serves 6-8

Date Bars

A crumble topping means that this fruity traybake looks as good as it tastes.

125g (4oz) plain flour

125g (4oz) rolled oats

90g (3oz) soft light brown sugar

125g (4oz) butter

Filling

280g (8oz) chopped dates

110ml (3½fl oz) water

1 tblspn caster sugar

2 tblspn lemon juice

1 Combine all the ingredients for the filling in a mixing bowl. Microwave on High for 3-4 minutes, stirring every minute, until the dates have softened and the mixture is thick. Allow to cool.

2 Mix the flour, oats and brown sugar in a bowl. Rub in the butter until the mixture resembles coarse breadcrumbs. Set aside a quarter of the mixture and press the rest onto the base of a greased 20cm (8in) square dish.

3 Microwave the crumb base for 3-5 minutes. Start on Medium, but reduce the power to Low if the base starts to bubble.

4 Spoon the cooled date filling over the cooked base, spreading it evenly to the edges. Sprinkle the reserved crumble mixture on top in an even layer.

5 Microwave on High for 8 minutes. Cool, then cut into slices to serve.

Makes 16

Variation

Use no-need-to-soak dried apricots instead of dates, if preferred. The easiest way to chop them up is with kitchen scissors. Dip the blades of the scissors in a jug of boiling water from time to time. This method also works well for dates.

Apple and Spice Loaf

155g (5oz) plain flour
185g (6oz) caster sugar
1 tspn bicarbonate of soda
1 tspn ground cinnamon
¼ tspn ground nutmeg
¼ tspn ground cloves
4 tblspn sunflower oil
185g (6oz) sweetened apple purée
125g (4oz) raisins (optional)
2 eggs
2 tspn lemon juice

1 Beat all the ingredients together in a large bowl until smooth. Base line a glass microwave loaf dish with nonstick baking paper, spoon in the cake mixture and level the surface. Cook on Medium for 9 minutes, giving the dish a quarter turn every 2 minutes if necessary.

2 Increase the power to High and microwave for 3-5 minutes or until fully cooked, continuing to turn the dish as before if a turntable has not been used. Stand for 5-10 minutes; cool on a wire rack. Add a glaze if liked.

Makes 1 loaf

Variation

Date nut teabread: Mix 185g (6oz) chopped dates, 1 teaspoon bicarbonate of soda and 185ml (6fl oz) boiling water in a bowl. Stand for 10 minutes, then add 185g (6oz) soft light brown sugar, 4 tablespoons corn oil, 1 egg and the grated rind of 1 orange. Stir in 185g (6oz) plain flour and 60g (2oz) chopped walnuts. Beat the mixture by hand, with a wooden spoon, for 1 minute. Bake as for the Apple Spice Loaf, allowing 8 minutes on Medium power, then 2-4 minutes on Medium.

Note: When cooking a rectangular loaf it may be necessary to shield the ends of the dish with narrow foil strips to prevent overcooking. Consult your microwave handbook.

Apple and Spice Loaf and Date Nut Teabread (top), Date Bars

45

Luscious Lemon Sponge

- *185g (6oz) butter or margarine, softened*
- *185g (6oz) caster sugar*
- *185g (6oz) self-raising flour*
- *½ tspn baking powder*
- *finely grated rind of 1 lemon*
- *3 eggs*
- *2-3 tblspn milk*
- *lemon curd to fill*

Lemon Frosting

- *1 tblspn softened butter or margarine*
- *1½ tblspn single cream, evaporated milk or milk*
- *1½ tspn lemon juice*
- *1 tspn grated lemon rind*
- *250g (8oz) icing sugar*
- *yellow food colouring (optional)*

1 Grease a 20cm (8in) soufflé dish. Base line with nonstick baking paper. In a mixing bowl, beat together the butter, caster sugar, flour, baking powder, lemon rind, eggs and enough of the milk to give a soft dropping consistency. Spoon into the dish.

2 Microwave on High for 7-9 minutes or until a skewer inserted in the centre comes out clean. If necessary, give the dish a quarter turn every 2 minutes to promote even cooking.

3 Leave the cake to stand in the dish for 10 minutes, then turn out on a wire rack, remove the paper and cool.

4 Meanwhile make the frosting by combining the butter, cream (or alternative), lemon juice and grated lemon rind together in a bowl. Microwave on Medium for 30-40 seconds or until mixture bubbles.

5 Add the icing sugar, with just enough colouring to tint the mixture a pale yellow, and beat until the frosting is of a spreading consistency.

6 Split the cake in half, sandwich with lemon curd, then cover the sides and top with the frosting.

Makes 1 cake

Luscious Lemon Sponge

USEFUL INFORMATION

Length

Centimetres	Inches	Centimetres	Inches
0.5 (5mm)	¼	18	7
1	½	20	8
2	¾	23	9
2.5	1	25	10
4	1½	30	12
5	2	35	14
6	2½	40	16
7.5	3	45	18
10	4	50	20
15	6	NB: 1cm = 10 mm	

Metric/Imperial Conversion Chart
Mass (Weight)
(Approximate conversions for cookery purposes)

Metric	Imperial	Metric	Imperial
15g	½oz	315g	10oz
30g	1oz	350g	11oz
60g	2oz	375g	12oz (¾lb)
90g	3oz	410g	13oz
125g	4oz (¼lb)	440g	14oz
155g	5oz	470g	15oz
185g	6oz	500g (0.5kg)	16oz (1lb)
220g	7oz	750g	24oz (1½lb)
250g	8oz (½lb)	1000g (1 kg)	32oz (2lb)
280g	9oz	1500g (1.5kg)	3lb

Metric Spoon Sizes

Metric Spoon Sizes

¼ teaspoon	= 1.25ml
½ teaspoon	= 2.5ml
1 teaspoon	= 5ml
1 tablespoon	=15ml

Liquids

Metric	Imperial
30ml	1 fl oz
60 ml	2fl oz
90ml	3fl oz
125ml	4fl oz
155ml	5fl oz (¼ pt)
185ml	6fl oz
250ml	8fl oz
500ml	16fl oz
600ml	20fl oz (1 pt)
750ml	1¼pt
1 litre	1¾pt
1.2 litres	2pt
1.5 litres	2½pt
1.8 litres	3pt
2 litres	3½pt
2.5 litres	4pt

Index

Editorial Coordination: Merehurst Limited
Cookery Editor: Jenni Fleetwood
Design: Clive Dorman
Cover Photography: David Gill
Cover Home Economist: Maxine Clark
Photography: pages 6,7,9,11,12,17,20,22,23,24,26,
33,35,36,38,40, 41,42 supplied by Marshall
Cavendish Picture Library, London; pages
2,3,5,10,14,19,21,27,28,31,32,44,45,46 supplied by
Cy DeCosse Incorporated, USA.

Published by J.B. Fairfax Press Pty Limited
80-82 McLachlan Avenue
Rushcutters Bay 2011

Printed by Toppan Printing Co, Singapore
PRINTED IN SINGAPORE

ISBN 1 86343 116 0 (set)
ISBN 1 86343 224 8

Distribution and Sales Enquiries
Australia: J.B. Fairfax Press Pty Limited
Tel: (02) 9361 6366 Fax: (02) 9360 6262
United Kingdom: J.B. Fairfax Press Limited
Tel: (01933) 402330 Fax: (01933) 402234